COVER: "TWO LITTLE CIRCUS GIRLS"

IS A TENDER AND DRAMATIC STUDY OF THE PROFESSIONAL POISE OF TWO YOUNG JUGGLERS AT THE MOMENT THEIR COURAGE IS BEING TESTED. ONE OF THE JUGGLERS HAS DROPPED HER ARMFUL OF ORANGES. HER ARMS HOLD EMPTY SPACE. SHE STUDIES THE REACTION OF THE AUDIENCE. HER PARTNER TURNS HER HEAD SLIGHTLY BUT KEEPS HER BALANCED POSITION.

THESE ARE PRACTICED PERFORMERS RENOIR HAS PAINTED. THE ORANGES WILL BE GATHERED UP AND THE ACT WILL GO ON.

LAUNDRESS AND CHILD   ETCHING, 1886
PRIVATE COLLECTION, CLEVELAND

A GIRL WITH A WATERING CAN   NATIONAL GALLERY OF ART, WASHINGTON, D.C., CHESTER DALE COLLECTION

DEDICATED TO THE RABOFF AND THE SONTAG FAMILIES

LIBRARY OF CONGRESS CATALOGING-IN-PUBLICATION DATA
RABOFF, ERNEST LLOYD
    PIERRE-AUGUSTE RENOIR
    (ART FOR CHILDREN)
    REPRINT. ORIGINALLY PUBLISHED: GARDEN CITY, N.Y.: DOUBLEDAY, 1970. SUMMARY: A BRIEF BIOGRAPHY OF PIERRE-AUGUSTE RENOIR AC-
COMPANIES FIFTEEN COLOR REPRODUCTIONS AND CRITICAL INTERPRETATIONS OF HIS WORKS. 1. RENOIR, AUGUSTE, 1841-1919 - JUVENILE LITERATURE.
2. PAINTERS - FRANCE - BIOGRAPHY - JUVENILE LITERATURE. 3. PAINTING, FRENCH - JUVENILE LITERATURE. 4. PAINTING, MODERN - 19TH CENTURY -
FRANCE - JUVENILE LITERATURE. 5. PAINTING, MODERN - 20TH CENTURY - FRANCE - JUVENILE LITERATURE. 6. IMPRESSIONISM (ART) - FRANCE -
JUVENILE LITERATURE. [1. RENOIR, AUGUSTE, 1841-1919. 2. ARTISTS. 3. PAINTING, FRENCH. 4. PAINTING, MODERN - 19TH CENTURY - FRANCE.
5. IMPRESSIONISM (ART)] I. TITLE II. SERIES. ND553.R45R3 1987   759.4   [92]   87-45154   ISBN 0-397-33217-8
    "A HARPER TROPHY BOOK."   ISBN 0-06-446068-1 (PBK.)   87-45145

PIERRE-AUGUSTE RENOIR

By Ernest Raboff

ART FOR CHILDREN

A HARPER TROPHY BOOK

HARPER & ROW, PUBLISHERS

PIERRE-AUGUSTE **RENOIR** (RAY-NEW AR')
WAS BORN ON FEBRUARY 25, 1841, IN LIMOGES, FRANCE.
HIS FATHER, LÉONARD, AND HIS MOTHER, MARGUERITE,
WORKED AS TAILOR AND DRESS MAKER TO EARN A LIVING
FOR THEIR FAMILY OF SEVEN CHILDREN.

WHEN HE WAS 13, YOUNG AUGUSTE WENT TO WORK AS AN
APPRENTICE IN THE ART OF DECORATING PORCELAIN DISHES.
HE LEARNED TO CREATE A VASE FROM CLAY ON THE POTTER'S
WHEEL, TO "FIRE" IT IN THE KILN, DECORATE IT WITH PAINT AND
FIRE IT AGAIN TO MAKE THE COLORS PERMANENT. BEFORE HE
WAS 20, HE HAD PAINTED 20 MURALS ON THE WALLS OF PARIS CAFES.

WHILE STILL A YOUNG MAN, RENOIR BECAME ONE OF THE FOUNDERS
OF THE IMPRESSIONIST MOVEMENT IN ART. OTHER IMPORTANT
IMPRESSIONIST PAINTERS WERE HIS CLOSE FRIENDS MONET,
SISLEY, CÉZANNE AND PISSARRO.

RENOIR SHOWED HIS ADMIRATION
FOR WOMEN IN MANY DRAWINGS,
PAINTINGS AND SCULPTURES. HIS
SOFTLY COLORFUL LANDSCAPES,
FLOWERS AND CHILDREN MAKE
SOME OF THE MOST JOYOUS
PAINTINGS IN THE HISTORY
OF ART.

RENOIR DRAWN BY ERNEST RABOFF

PIERRE-AUGUSTE RENOIR SAID:

"YOU SHOULD LET PEOPLE GET THE BETTER OF YOU! IF YOU DON'T FIGHT, YOU DISARM THEM. THEN THEY BECOME NICE — BUT YOU MUST GIVE THEM A CHANCE."

RENOIR BELIEVED THAT EVERY HUMAN BEING SHOULD MAKE OR DO SOMETHING WITH HIS HANDS EVERY DAY. "AFTER ALL", HE NOTED, "I WORK WITH MY HANDS AND THAT MAKES ME A WORKING MAN, A WORK-MAN PAINTER."

"THE ARTIST WHO USES THE LEAST OF WHAT IS CALLED IMAGINATION WILL BE THE GREATEST. TO BE AN ARTIST YOU MUST LEARN TO KNOW THE LAWS OF NATURE."

"THE ONLY REWARD FOR WORK IS THE WORK ITSELF."

"WHEN ONE PICTURE IS FINISHED I LONG TO BEGIN THE NEXT."

SELF-PORTRAIT, ABOUT AGE 35   FOGG ART MUSEUM, HARVARD UNIVERSITY, MAURICE WERTHEIM COLLECTION

"BOUQUET OF SPRING FLOWERS," PAINTED BY AUGUSTE RENOIR WHEN HE WAS 25 YEARS OLD, DISPLAYS A DAZZLING VARIETY OF FLOWERS.

EVERY BLOSSOM, EVERY PETAL, EVERY STEM AND DETAILED LEAF IS ALIVE AND VIBRATING WITH BRIGHT, SPARKLING INDIVIDUALITY.

IT IS A GARDEN OF COLORS GATHERED INTO A SINGLE VASE.

MAKE BELIEVE THAT YOUR EYES CAN WALK. START AT THE LOWER LEFT CORNER AND TAKE A STROLL UPWARD THROUGH THIS FLORAL WONDERLAND.

ONE CAN ALMOST SMELL THE FRAGRANT SCENTS RISING FROM THE FLOWERS AND ALMOST IMAGINE A BEE'S BUZZING APPROACH IN SEARCH OF HONEY.

RENOIR'S LOVE FOR THE TIME IN HIS YOUTH WHEN HE WAS A PAINTER OF PORCELAIN IS RECAPTURED IN THIS BEAUTIFULLY DECORATED BLUE VASE.

BOUQUET OF SPRING FLOWERS, 1866   FOGG ART MUSEUM, HARVARD UNIVERSITY,   GRENVILLE L. WINTHROP BEQUEST

"LADY WITH A PARASOL" IS A SHIMMERING IMPRESSION OF A LOVELY DAY AS THE HEAT OF THE SUN SENDS ITS RAYS RIPPLING ACROSS THE LANDSCAPE.

PICTURES SUCH AS THIS ONE WERE CALLED "OPEN AIR" PAINTINGS. FOR THE FIRST TIME, PAINTINGS WERE COMPLETED ENTIRELY OUTSIDE OF THE STUDIO. THEIR EXCITING BURSTS OF COLOR REFLECTING THE REAL OUTDOORS CREATED A WHOLE NEW SCHOOL OF PAINTING WHICH WAS CALLED IMPRESSIONISM.

RENOIR AND HIS FRIENDS CLAUDE MONET, ALFRED SISLEY, JEAN BAZILLE, CAMILLE PISSARRO, PAUL CÉZANNE AND ÉDOUARD MANET WERE KNOWN AS IMPRESSIONISTS.

THEIR NEW WAY OF SEEING BROUGHT THE OUTDOORS TO THE LIVING ROOM WALL. INTO THE HOME CAME THE MOVEMENT OF GRASS BENDING IN THE BREEZE, THE GLEAM OF SUNLIGHT BOUNCING OFF A PARASOL AND REFLECTING IN A CHILD'S GOLDEN HAIR.

ANGLERS ALONG THE SEINE, DETAIL

LADY WITH A PARASOL   MUSEUM OF FINE ARTS, BOSTON, BEQUEST OF JOHN T. SPAULDING

"OARSMEN AT CHATOU" CHALLENGES OUR EYES TO A RACE ON A SHIMMERING RIVER, PAST PEOPLE, OARSMEN AND BOATS. ACROSS THE BLUE BAY A CLUSTER OF RED-ROOFED HOUSES BASKS IN THE SUN.

THE ENTIRE PAINTING IS BATHED IN BLUE LIGHT. IT IS ON THE RIPPLING WATER, ON THE SAIL OF A BOAT, IN THE MEADOW BORDERING THE RIVER AND ON THE WHITE JACKET AND SHIRT.

RED, GREEN, BLUE, YELLOW AND PURPLE PERFORM THEIR OWN RACE AROUND THE CANVAS.

HEAD OF A YOUNG GIRL (STUDY FOR PAINTING "GIRL READING")
PRIVATE COLLECTION, HOLLAND

OUR IMPRESSION IS OF A BEAUTIFUL SUMMER DAY. THE BREEZE RUFFLES THE SURFACE OF THE WATER, FILLING THE BILLOWING SAIL AND SCATTERING THE LOW-LYING CLOUDS.

AUGUSTE RENOIR'S EYES, HAND AND BRUSH RECORDED A FLEETING MOMENT FOREVER.

OARSMEN AT CHATOU   NATIONAL GALLERY OF ART, WASHINGTON, D.C. , GIFT OF SAM A. LEWISOHN

IN "LADY SEWING" RENOIR FLOODS AN INTERIOR
SCENE WITH OUTDOOR LIGHT, CREATING A MASTERPIECE
OF IMPRESSIONISM.

PIANO STUDY, BUDAPEST MUSEUM OF FINE ARTS

THE
BOUQUET OF FLOWERS,
THE STURDY VASE
AND
THE WOMAN SEWING
ARE BATHED
IN THE SUNLIGHT
COMING THROUGH
THE WINDOW
FROM THE UPPER RIGHT.

THE ARTIST CREATES AN INTERESTING STUDY OF
CONTRASTS BETWEEN THE TRANQUILLITY OF THE WOMAN
AND THE BRIGHT, VIBRATING COLORS OF THE FLOWERS.

THE WOMAN IS OCCUPIED WITH A QUIET, DOMESTIC
CHORE, BUT SHE IS PROBABLY THE SAME PERSON WHO
SELECTED AND PLACED THE VIBRANT FLOWERS. THEIR
EXCITING ARRANGEMENT MAKES THIS PICTURE SPARKLE
LIKE

A JEWEL.

LADY SEWING, 1879   THE ART INSTITUTE OF CHICAGO,   MR. AND MRS. L.L. COBURN MEMORIAL COLLECTION

IN "MOTHER AND CHILD"
THE PAINTER PIERRE-AUGUSTE RENOIR
WAS ABLE TO PUT HIS TALENT FOR PAINTING
FORMS REALISTICALLY AND SENSITIVELY INTO
HIS MOLDING OF CLAY AND WAX FORMS.
THESE SCULPTURES WERE CAST IN BRONZE TO BECOME
THE MAGNIFICENT BRONZE WORKS OF
THE SCULPTOR PIERRE-AUGUSTE RENOIR.

HIS FAVORITE SUBJECTS FOR SCULPTURE WERE
WOMEN AND CHILDREN. HIS WIFE, ALINE, AND HIS SONS,
PIERRE, CLAUDE AND
JEAN, WERE OFTEN
THE ARTIST'S MODELS.

LANDSCAPE AND FIGURES, DETAIL, THE DETROIT INSTITUTE OF ARTS

BUT HIS MOST FAMOUS
MODEL FOR BOTH
PAINTING AND SCULPTURE
WAS HIS COUSIN,
GABRIELLE RENARD.

STUDY THE SOFT
REALISM IN THIS
METAL SCULPTURE
OF MOTHER AND CHILD.

MOTHER AND CHILD   THE PHILLIPS COLLECTION , WASHINGTON, D.C.

"LUNCHEON OF THE BOATING PARTY" IS A SLOWLY
SPINNING CAROUSEL OF BLUES AND GOLDS. OUR GAZE MOVES
AROUND AND AROUND THE TABLE LADEN WITH BOTTLES,
GLASSES AND FRUIT, AND ENCIRCLED BY MEN IN SHIRT SLEEVES
AND JACKETS, WOMEN IN DRESSES AND BONNETS. OUR EYES
REST ON THE GIRL IN THE FLOWERED HAT HOLDING A DOG.
SHE IS ALINE CHARIGOT, WHO LATER BECAME RENOIR'S WIFE.

IN THE UPPER RIGHT CORNER A CIRCLE IS FORMED BY TWO
MEN AND A WOMAN. STILL ANOTHER IS FORMED IN THE
FAR CENTER BEGINNING WITH THE BEARDED MAN IN
THE TOP HAT AND INCLUDING THE MAN FACING US IN THE
BLUE CAP, THE WOMAN LEANING ON THE RAIL AND THE
MAN IN THE BROWN HAT. THIS CIRCLE IS COMPLETED

ED. RENOIR IN MENTON   PAUL ROSENBERG COL.

BY THE GIRL HOLDING A GLASS
TO HER LIPS. THE FIVE ORANGE-
GOLD HATS INTERWEAVE
THE LIVELY CIRCLES.

THESE PEOPLE WERE THE
ARTIST'S FRIENDS. RENOIR
USED THE BACKGROUND OF
LACY BRANCHES AND THE
PALE REFLECTION OF SUN-
LIGHT TO BIND THE PICTURE
SOFTLY TOGETHER.

THE LUNCHEON OF THE BOATING PARTY   THE PHILLIPS COLLECTION , WASHINGTON, D.C.

"FRUITS FROM THE MIDI" PRESENTS ANOTHER IMPRESSIONIST WORK THAT KEEPS OUR ATTENTION MOVING BETWEEN INTERESTING FORMS AND GLOWING COLOR.

CHOOSE A COLOR AND TRACE ITS PATH FROM TOP TO BOTTOM OF THE PAINTING, THEN FROM SIDE TO SIDE AND AROUND THE TABLE.

RENOIR FILLS THE ENTIRE CANVAS WITH LIGHT. HIS FRUITS AND VEGETABLES SPARKLE AND GLITTER. THEY HAVE THEIR OWN SPECIAL HUES. THE LIGHTER ONES PICK UP REDS AND GREENS MIRRORED IN THEIR SHINING SIDES.

EVEN THE BLUE BACKGROUND IS ALIVE WITH MOVING BRUSH STROKES. IT REFLECTS ALL THE COLORS OF THE LEAVES, THE FRUITS, THE SUNLIGHT AND SKY.

ARGENTEUIL, DETAIL   EDITH WETMORE COLLECTION, NEW YORK

FRUITS FROM THE MIDI, 1881   THE ART INSTITUTE OF CHICAGO, MR. AND MRS. MARTIN A. RYERSON COLLECTION

"L'ESTAQUE" WAS A FAVORITE LANDSCAPE
SCENE FOR RENOIR AND HIS FRIEND PAUL CÉZANNE.
THEY OFTEN WENT THERE TOGETHER TO PAINT.

IN THIS RICH AND BEAUTIFUL EXAMPLE OF
IMPRESSIONISM, RENOIR'S BRUSH TOUCHES EVERY
OBJECT WITH A SPRINKLING RAIN OF COLOR.

BRIGHT AND HAPPY DASHES OF PAINT FROM HIS
PALETTE CREATE A RAINBOW ON A TUFT OF GRASS,
OVER A YOUNG TREE TRUNK, ON A TWIG BURSTING WITH
LEAVES AND ACROSS THE COOL SHADOWS STRIPING
THE ROAD. HIS BRUSH HAS WOVEN A CARPET OF
COLORS OVER THE ENTIRE CANVAS.

STUDY FOR THE PORTRAIT OF JULIE MANET WITH HER CAT
COLLECTION OF MME. ERNEST ROUART, PARIS

THE SKY AND THE
SEA BELOW IT
ARE STITCHED TOGETHER
BY THE THREAD OF THE
HORIZON.

ARTISTS ARE LIKE
TEACHERS IN THE
ART OF SEEING__
AND OUR EYES HAVE
MUCH TO LEARN.

L'ESTAQUE   MUSEUM OF FINE ARTS, BOSTON, JULIANA CHENEY EDWARDS COLLECTION

"THE UMBRELLAS" IS A FASCINATING STUDY THAT SHOWS RENOIR'S ABILITY TO SOFTEN COLORS AND LIGHTS WHILE KEEPING A WARMTH FLOWING THROUGHOUT THE PAINTING.

PORTRAIT OF LOUIS VALTAT

HIS TALENT AS A PORTRAIT PAINTER IS SHOWN IN THE HEADS OF THE TWO WOMEN, THE CHILD WITH THE HOOP AND THE MAN ON THE LEFT IN THE PICTURE.

RENOIR'S FACES SHINE FROM THE CANVAS WITH A PEACE AND CONTENTMENT.

THE UMBRELLAS CREATE A MELODY OF MOVEMENT THAT IS SOFT AND BEAUTIFUL LIKE THE SOUND OF RAIN DROPPING ON THE LEAVES OF A TREE.

THE SHAPES OF THE WOODEN BASKET, THE HOOP AND STICK HELD BY THE CHILD AND THE STAFFS OF THE UMBRELLAS PLAY IN AND AROUND THE PAINTING LIKE ARROWS DIRECTING US FROM ONE SCENE TO ANOTHER.

THE UMBRELLAS   THE NATIONAL GALLERY, LONDON, COURTESY OF THE TRUSTEES

"DANCE AT BOUGIVAL" WAS PAINTED TWO YEARS
AFTER RENOIR'S MARRIAGE TO ALINE CHARIGOT.
LIKE ALL OF HIS WORK, THIS ONE IS FILLED WITH
TENDERNESS AND ROMANCE.

HOW LOVELY AND GRACEFUL IS THE YOUNG LADY IN
HER RED BONNET AND WHITE SWIRLING DRESS!

HOW FIRMLY HER PARTNER IN HIS YELLOW HAT HOLDS HER
TO HIM WHILE HE STUDIES HER LOVELY FACE! WE
ARE CAUGHT UP IN THE HARMONY OF THE MOMENT.

NOTICE HOW RENOIR USES THE FLOWING COLORS OF
IMPRESSIONISM
ALL AROUND THE DANCING COUPLE JUST AS THE
PETALS OF A FLOWER FORM A FRAME FOR ITS
CENTER.

DANCE AT BOUGIVAL   MUSEUM OF FINE ARTS, BOSTON, PICTURE FUND

GIRL WITH A SICKLE, DETAIL

"IN THE MEADOW" IS A PAINTING OF YOUTH AND SPRING. IT IS THE CHILDHOOD SEASON FOR THE GRASS AND LEAVES. EVEN THE SKY IS BREAK-OF-DAY BLUE.

THE MILD SUN CASTS A WARM GLOW ACROSS THE DISTANT HILL, ON THE STROLLERS DOWN THE PATH, THROUGH THE MEADOW AND ON THE GRASSY KNOLL WITH ITS FEATHERY BUSHES IN FRONT OF THE TWO GIRLS.

RENOIR LEADS US THROUGH THE PAINTING ON TRAILS OF COLOR. THE ARM OF THE GIRL IN THE ROSE DRESS LEADS US TO THE ROSE-RED SHADOW BELOW THE TREE ON THE RIGHT, AND TO THE GOLDEN-HAIRED GIRL HOLDING MEADOW FLOWERS. THEY FRAME THE DISTANT LANDSCAPE.

IN THE MEADOW   THE METROPOLITAN MUSEUM OF ART, BEQUEST OF SAMUEL A. LEWISOHN, 1951

TWO DRAWINGS OF PIERRE RENOIR, C. 1896

"A SHEPHERD BOY" IS ONE OF AUGUSTE RENOIR'S MASTERPIECES WHICH DEMONSTRATES HIS TALENTS AS A PAINTER AND REVEALS HIS PHILOSOPHY OF ART.

THE SHEPHERD, RESTING AGAINST A FALLEN LOG, IS SET LIKE A CLASSICAL SCULPTURE IN A GARDEN OF FLOWERS, TREES AND BIRDS. IN HIS LEFT HAND HE HOLDS A GOLDEN FLUTE TO PLAY HIS CAREFREE TUNES. HIS RIGHT HAND IS ABOUT TO BECOME A PERCH FOR A BIRD THAT PERHAPS HEARD THE MUSIC OF HIS PIPE.

RENOIR WAS A ROMANTIC POET SPEAKING WITH PAINT. RHYTHMS IN HIS CANVAS VERSES ARE THE MOVEMENTS OF HIS BRUSH STROKES. HIS RHYMES ARE HIS RICH AND HARMONIOUS COLORS. HIS THOUGHTS ARE REVEALED IN THE FACES HE PAINTS, THE GRACE OF HIS ROUNDED FORMS AND THE BEAUTY OF HIS SUBJECTS.

A SHEPHERD BOY   MUSEUM OF ART, RHODE ISLAND SCHOOL OF DESIGN

CHILD DOING NEEDLE-WORK, 1895-1900